Coaching Emotional Intelligence

A foundation for HR Professionals,
Internal Coaches, Trainers and Consultants

Joseph Liberti

Coaching Emotional Intelligence

ISBN 978-0-557-19197-0

Table of Contents

Chapter 1: Introduction 1

Chapter 2: Emotional Intelligence Inside 3

Chapter 3: A Focus On Core EI Skills 9

Chapter 4: Preparing To Launch - 5 Key Questions....................11

Chapter 5: Getting Buy-In..15

Chapter 6: Features and Benefits of Emotional Intelligence 19

Chapter 7: An EQ Development Plan 23

Chapter 8: What Didn't Work; What Did......................................29

Chapter 9: About Emotional Intelligence Assessments...............35

Chapter 10: The Introductory Presentation...................................41

Chapter 11: What Is An EQ Coach? 45

Chapter 12: Required Coach Competencies 49

Chapter 13: The EQ Coaching Process 53

Chapter 14: Who To Coach; Who Not..59

Chapter 15: But, Will They Like It? 63

Chapter 16: Group Coaching..65

Chapter 17: The Influential Difference 69

Chapter 18: What About Coach Certification 75

Chapter 19: A Successful EQ Coaching Career? 79

Chapter 20: How EQ Improves Coaching And Training Results 83

Chapter 21: What Is The Best Development Approach For You? 89

Appendix: Assessments and Resources 93

Chapter 1: Introduction

Are you preparing to coach or train emotional intelligence?

There's no question that emotional intelligence, a set of skills that enable people to better manage themselves and others, works. Research and case studies have proven that emotional intelligence can be developed and when it is, the results are: improved performance, reduced stress and a more enjoyable and cooperative work environment. But where do you start?

Whether you are:

- ✓ An internal coach with a responsibility to improve workplace harmony and effectiveness
- ✓ A consultant or trainer who wants to help leaders and teams develop more people skills
- ✓ An experienced coach looking for a niche or if you are
- ✓ Just thinking of becoming a coach

You probably have questions about developing emotional intelligence and how to get started as an EQ Coach or trainer.

This book answers frequently asked questions and will help you identify what you need to know, have and do to be a confident, competent and successful emotional intelligence coach and to launch an EQ training initiative in an organization.

Hello, I'm Joseph Liberti, President and founder of EQ At Work.

I coach leaders and coaches to develop emotional intelligence. I have specialized in developing emotional intelligence for 15 years and I have performed over 4000 hours of emotional intelligence coaching. My company, EQ At Work, established in 1998, trains and certifies EQ coaches and trainers and provides emotional intelligence consulting and training to individuals and organizations.

Since 1998, my EQ At Work Method™ has been used to develop the emotional competency and leadership ability of hundreds of people in large and small organizations including: Allstate Insurance, Blue Cross/Blue Shield, Boeing, Eli Lilly, Healthways, IBM, NPR, Northrop Aviation, Payless Shoes, Pfizer, Social Security Administration, St Mary's Hospitals, University of Southern CA, US Department of Labor, the US Postal Service and St Mary's Hospitals.

In this book I share experience and insights gleaned from 20 years of training and coaching. I also give you some cutting edge concepts and strategies about emotional intelligence and some practical tips for EQ coaching and training success. You will also find links to valuable resources. For convenience in writing and reading, I will use the designations EQ and EI interchangeably as abbreviations for emotional intelligence in this book.

It is my pleasure to share my knowledge and passion with you.

Joseph Liberti

Chapter 2: Emotional Intelligence Inside

Today's Emotional intelligence has its roots in the social behavioral research of the 30s, 40's and 50's. The concept was further advanced by various researchers including: Howard Gardner, with his Multiple Intelligence theory, introduced in 1975; Reuven Bar-On who was the first to quantify EQ, or emotional quotient; and John Mayer and Peter Salovey who published a landmark article called Emotional Intelligence, in 1990.

It was psychologist and New York Times science writer Daniel Coleman, however, who brought emotional intelligence into the mainstream with his best-selling 1995 book Emotional Intelligence: Why It Can Matter More Than IQ.

Definition

What is emotional intelligence?

Simply put: **emotional intelligence is a set of skills that enable you to more effectively manage yourself and relate with others.**

While there are many models and measures of EQ, Goleman's emotional competency model became the popular way to represent emotional intelligence and presents four domains of emotional competency, and within each domain related competencies. For a detailed view with definitions see:

http://www.eiconsortium.org/measures/eci_360.html

The table on the next page shows a condensed version of The Goleman model.

Goleman's Emotional Competency Model

Self-Awareness

Emotional self-Awareness

Realistic self-assessment

Self-Management

Emotional self-control

Adaptability

Achievement orientation

Positive outlook

Social Awareness

Empathy

Organizational awareness

Relationship Management

Inspirational leadership

Influence

Conflict management

Teamwork

Emotional Competency

What is an emotional competency? Competencies are the set of behaviors which drive outstanding performance in a given job, role or function. Since the early 1970's, leading organizations have been using competencies to help recruit, select and manage their outstanding performers.

Goleman adopted the competency model as a framework for emotional skills. As Goleman defined the term in *Working With Emotional Intelligence* 1998, "Emotional Competence is a learned capability, based on emotional intelligence, that results in outstanding performance at work." For example, trustworthiness, listed in the domain of self-Management in Goleman's model, is an emotional competence based on the emotional skill of self-regulation, or managing impulses and emotions well.

Different Models and Measures - Common Core Skills

It is important to recognize that while the models of Mayer and Salovey, Bar-On, Goleman and others have differences, they have similarities too. They all share common, essential emotional skills. These core skills are the emotional intelligence upon which Goleman's competencies are based and include the ability to: *Perceive, Understand, Express, Manage and Influence emotions.*

Increase Training Effectiveness: Develop Core Skills

In developing emotional intelligence you can increase coaching and training effectiveness by beginning with a focus on the development of core skills. (See *Chapter 3: A Focus On Core Skills*) Then you can support learners to apply the core skills on the job in emotionally competent behavior. In the example used earlier on trustworthiness an underlying core skill is managing emotions.

Emotional Skills - Interdependent and Hierarchical

The skills of emotional intelligence are both interdependent and hierarchical.

It is important to recognize the relationship between emotional skills.   I have heard some consultants advise clients to improve the skill that they scored lowest on in an EQ assessment. (More about assessment in Chapter 9) They might say: "well, you scored lower on empathy, that's what you need to develop."

> **Selecting only one emotional skill to develop cannot be wholly effective because each emotional skill is dependent on another. For example, emotional self-management is dependent on emotional awareness, the foundation of all other emotional skills.**

Obviously, your ability to manage your emotions is dependent on your ability to be aware of which emotions are influencing you. Less obvious is that empathy, a skill in the domain of social awareness, is dependent on self-awareness.

My experience is that people's ability to recognize and understand the emotions of others is dependent on their ability to do that with themselves. For example, the degree to which I am able to empathize with someone else's sadness is dependent on the degree to which I am able to recognize and accept my own sadness.

> **Because of the interdependence of emotional skills, overall emotional intelligence is best learned from the bottom up.**

The most effective approach is to start by developing self-awareness, advancing to self-management, then to the skill of awareness of others and finally putting it all together in the skills of relationship.

To prepare yourself to facilitate the development of emotional intelligence, you need to:

Know

✓ There are different models and measures of emotional intelligence.

✓ Workplace emotional competencies are dependent on core emotional skills, including the ability to perceive, understand, manage, express and influence emotions. (See Chapter 3 for specific skills)

✓ Emotional skills are interdependent and hierarchical.

Have

✓ An understanding of the workplace competencies your client wishes to improve, so that you can relate them to core emotional skills.

Do

✓ Develop your own emotional skills to effectively support others.

✓ Consider hiring your own experienced, skillful EQ coach.

Chapter 3: A Focus On Core EI Skills

I like to focus on the development of core emotional skills, to enable lasting positive change of behaviors by coaching at the level of cause. How does that work? I'll use time management as an example issue to be clear.

If I was your coach and you wanted to improve your ability to manage time, I could suggest you get a new calendar or iPhone, and tell you to use it to stay on time. You might try it for a while but soon fall victim to the same old habits. Or I could tell you to use author David Allen's task management method to prioritize and get things done. You might give this a try too, and you might even make some improvement, but not really solve your problem. Why? Because if they are not dealt with, the most powerful influence on your time management, the emotions that influence your behavior, would still sabotage your results.

Coaching with emotional intelligence, I could support you to recognize how your emotions are influencing the choices you make that cause you to be late. For example: One client, I worked with, couldn't say no, constantly overcommitted, and as a result was always overwhelmed and late. When he was able to become aware of and manage his fear of losing approval, he finally got a grip on his commitments, his time and his life.

> **The core emotional skills that enable competency and increased personal effectiveness include the ability to: Perceive, Understand, Manage, Express and Influence emotions.**

I have created a simple online questionnaire to help you evaluate your command of core emotional intelligence skills and to provide an example of a simple, yet useful assessment tool.

This simple questionnaire lists ten core emotional skills. It is not scientifically validated and is not intended to be an absolute measure of your emotional intelligence, but is useful in recognizing your present level of competence and setting goals for your development. Be as objective and realistic as you can be. Save your results. Later you can complete a second questionnaire (or several) and evaluate your progress.

A link to the Emotional Skills Questionnaire is in the Appendix of this book..

Regarding core emotional skills, what you need to:

Know

- ✓ Core emotional skills include the ability to perceive, understand, manage, express and influence emotions.

- ✓ Developing core emotional skills enables workplace competency. For example, highly effective communication is enabled by your skill in recognizing emotions in others. If you know what they are feeling you can modify your message to positively influence their state and create greater understanding.

- ✓ As a coach or trainer, development of your own core skills enables you get to help others understand and manage the emotions that influence their thinking and action.

Have

- ✓ Clear goals and plans for developing your own core emotional skills. For example, do you want to improve your ability to recognize your emotions in the moment from sometimes to almost always? How will you do that?

Do

- ✓ In conducting coaching and training, begin with identifying workplace competencies you want to improve, in your clients, and relate them to the underlying core emotional skills.

Chapter 4: Preparing To Launch - 5 Key Questions

Are you an HR professional considering an emotional intelligence development initiative for your organization? Or, maybe you are a coach or trainer who's been asked to introduce emotional intelligence in your company or a client organization. As you prepare to launch, what things do you need to consider? What questions do you need to ask? To help you organize for success, let's consider the challenge my client Rob was facing.

"We are having an executive retreat for 60 of our top leaders and the president has asked me to provide a program about emotional intelligence," he said. "The company has hired a high profile, dynamic speaker to present the keynote and I am on the program just before him. I've got to deliver a great presentation to a resistant audience or fall flat on my face. How can you help me?"

Rob was the Vice President of Human Resources for a large agricultural services company and had been referred to me by a client. I typically get calls like Rob's in late Spring and am sometimes hired to present introductory EQ programs at retreats and conferences. In this case, the president had told Bob, "We need more of that emotional intelligence around here." He asked Rob to make the presentation at the retreat, as part of the management team, and take the lead in bringing emotional intelligence into the company.

Rob was fortunate to get such support and he was already passionately interested in the subject but he felt really challenged. "We have Mensa level talent here, he said, but they have little emotional skill and often ride roughshod over employees, discouraging participation and performance." "And," he went on, "they are really resistant to any of that touchy feely stuff."

After all my years in the emotional intelligence business I'd like to think that the expression "touchy feely" has gone away, but it hasn't. To my judgmental brain it sounds as anachronistic as "those confounded horseless carriages." But I suspend judgment and I listen carefully with mind and heart. I realize those words are a defense to cover up the fear of dealing with emotions - one's own and others. And listening to Rob, it was obvious that while he may be dealing with a resistant audience, his own unexpressed fears were a bigger barrier to a successful presentation.

I consulted with Rob to help him prepare for the retreat, and his presentation was a smash hit. He used the information and materials and strategies I gave him to great advantage, but I am clear that the greatest support I gave him was helping him to manage his own emotions instead of projecting his fear onto his audience. His self-management enabled him to be present, let his passion come through and be powerful and effective.

5 Key Questions To Ask Yourself

I acknowledge Rob for delivering a successful presentation. He got buy in for continuing development of EI in his organization. One of the things that helped him be successful was getting clear on what he wanted and taking the necessary actions to get it - from hiring a coach to thoroughly preparing and practicing. What supported Rob was my 5 key questions method, and it will help you too!

During our first conversation I asked Rob 5 key questions to support him to clarity and for me to understand how best to help him. I created this question process years ago and have always found it powerful and effective.

When I am meeting a new client I always ask the 5 key questions that I asked Rob. They are great questions to ask yourself about becoming an EQ coach or about any undertaking, and of course, great questions for you to ask clients.

I use the metaphor of a journey to help clients visualize outcomes. If you are in a situation similar to Rob's, charged with the responsibility, of leading a EQ development initiative in your organization, be sure to ask and answer these 5 key questions for yourself:

1. **Where are you going and why?** What is your ultimate destination or goal? What is so important about you getting there?

2. **How will you know when you get there?** In other words, how will you recognize success? What behaviors will you observe? What will you see or hear?

3. **What's In your way?** What are the challenges you face? What might stop you - from outside or from within?

4. **What will you need to learn or let go of?** What skill will you need to develop or bring to the fore? What beliefs or behaviors will you need to let go of?

5. **What steps will you take?** What action will you take towards your destination and what's next?

Rob's Example

To give you an example of how you might benefit from this method, here's how Rob answered those questions:

Q: Where are you going?

Rob: "My ultimate goal is to change the culture in our organization. We are so great intellectually. We can be fantastic if we use emotional intelligence and I want to see us be that great. My immediate goal is to hit a home run with the retreat presentation and maintain my influence as a member of the team."

Q: How will you know when you get there?

Rob: "At the end of my presentation I will hear people asking me how they can get more information and participate in our training. As we develop EQ in the organization I will hear people talking to each other with sensitivity and respect. I will see staff, at all levels, totally engaged and enthusiastically participating in projects."

Q: What's in your way?

Rob: "One challenge is to create a balance in our people, between the logical and the emotional. Not just have Mensa level intelligence but also have people be able to work with their heart. And another is to overcome resistance to dealing with emotions, in me and in my audience."

Q: What will you need to learn or let go of?

Rob: "I will have to learn about emotional intelligence and how to present it. I will need to let go of my belief that they don't want to hear it."

Q: What steps will you take?

Rob: "The first step is to get buy in with my presentation. Next we will conduct Lunch and Learn presentations to recruit people for EI training and development. Next we will integrate EQ in our leadership training, and finally in other training."

How would you answer these questions? How will your answers help you?

See Chapter 5 to understand more how to get buy-in and Chapter 10 on using introductory workshops, to learn more about successful presentations.

To Have a successful launch you need to:

Know

- ✓ Where you are going and why, what will stop you and what you need to learn.

Have

- ✓ Passion, commitment and courage.

Do

- ✓ Get clear on your next steps and take positive action.

Chapter 5: Getting Buy-In

...How to create interest and acceptance for the development of emotional intelligence in your organization

You see the possibilities. You recognize that your organization has capable and experienced people with great potential. And you see opportunities for gains where a lack of people skills is sabotaging results. You believe in emotional intelligence and you find yourself saying, with some longing and frustration, "How do I get past the resistance people express that emotional intelligence is too "touchy-feely" and doesn't belong in our workplace?"

In the last 15 years I have heard that question hundreds of times. At first I believed that the question would fade away as more and more case study evidence became available that emotional intelligence, also referred to as EQ, does have a positive impact on the bottom line. Yet while more and more people accepted EQ as valuable in business, there are still a very large number of people and organizations, who cling to the traditional thinking that emotions don't belong in business.

If you are asking yourself how to overcome this resistance, I have some answers for you. Here are five things to consider and ways to get started.

1. **Don't Take It Personally:** The touchy-feely complaint is not personal or even sensible; it's resistance to change. All of us have many years of social conditioning to overcome. We have been told many times that we shouldn't cry or "say something nice or not at all," or frequently in business, "leave your emotions at the door." And we were not trained to use emotions to inform our decisions but rather to regard emotions as a sign of weakness. With that history, of course

people are going to do their best to avoid dealing with emotions. Don't react to this expression; facilitate understanding.

2. **You Can't Reason With Them:** One of the reasons that many change initiatives fail is that the change agents only tried to communicate with logic and "give em the WIFM," the what's in it for me. They tried to explain what was going to be so good about the change - to convince people with reasoning that change was a good idea. Successful change requires that people's emotions be acknowledged and validated. As a facilitator you must provide enough "left brain food" to keep the mind busy while you demonstrate emotional intelligence by dealing with feelings - with understanding and validation. You may think you must show statistics and bottom line proof. While that is helpful, it is an emotional experience of the benefits that will actually move people to action.

3. **Begin With The End In Mind**: Where do you want to end up? Do you want to serve up the idea of the month, improve leadership, or transform the company culture? If you are clear on your objective and committed to it, your intention will help you influence minds and hearts. What is your plan for introducing EQ? I have talked with many who want to hold an introductory talk or program in the hopes of making a good impression and creating interest but have no idea of where they are going next. Have a next step in mind. Maybe your next step is a series of "lunch and learn" programs. Maybe it is to assess the leaders. Maybe it is to conduct an initial emotional intelligence training program with thought leaders. Use your first activity to feed the next activity.

4. **Get Out Of The Way:** This is not about you. The subject of emotional intelligence may seem personal, and you may fear rejection. You may get timid and apologetic about presenting emotional intelligence. This is the time to remember it's not about you - it is about and for them. You will need to deal with your own emotions and have the courage of your convictions. If you are reactive you will come across as defensive and you will undermine the value of the message. You don't need to be a guru or an expert in emotional

intelligence to be an effective facilitator of learning and change. You do need to be transparent and available, and be present to the needs and concerns of others.

5. **Sharpen Your Saw:** There's no question that the absolute best way to develop emotional intelligence in others is to demonstrate emotional competency yourself. If you really want to be a change agent then prepare yourself with study and practice and learn a system for developing EQ in yourself and others. It is no accident that you are the one who is thinking of leading the way to greater awareness in your organization. As the saying goes, "we teach what we need to learn." Embrace your role and your learning. You will be an inspiration to others.

To get buy-in, what you need to:

Know

✓ People's emotional resistance to change is triggered by a misperception of the change as threat. What they say and do, when they are reactive, is not logical, and it's not personal. Dealing with emotions, for many, is unconsciously perceived as a threat.

Have

✓ Clear objectives for emotional intelligence development for your client, team or organization, and a plan - before you begin.

Do

✓ Seek first to understand and validate people's emotions to open their ears to your message.

✓ Don't you, be the limiting factor. Mange your own emotions so you can effectively respond instead of react.

Chapter 6: Features and Benefits of Emotional Intelligence

...Don't sell the steak, sell the sizzle.

I have long ago forgotten where I heard that expression. It was sometime in my teens when I was going through a sales training class. The catchy phrase was meant to remind me that people don't buy the product; they buy what it will do for them. And, at the deepest level how they will feel when the product delivers as wished.

> **In preparing to coach and train emotional intelligence it is important to recognize that people won't buy into emotional intelligence for the concept but for what it will do for them.**

What problems will EQ competencies solve? How will performance or life be better? The best way for you to get your message across is to be able to express EQ in terms of features and benefits.

A feature is a distinguishing characteristic. A benefit is the specific advantage and/or pleasure that feature delivers. Here are a few examples of features and benefits of emotional intelligence that relate to the workplace.

Category: Leadership

EI Feature: The competency of emotional awareness of others enables a keen understanding of what people's needs and concerns are and what motivates their behavior.

EI Benefit: Leadership, experts say, is all about influence. When a leader really understands what is motivating people he or she can more precisely say and do what will influence those people to take positive action.

Category: Change Management

EI Feature: The competency of emotional self-management enables change leaders to respond instead of react to strongly stimulating situations.

EI Benefit: Change engenders strong emotions. With emotional self-management, instead of reacting and becoming part of the problem, change leaders will be able to acknowledge people's emotions but remain calm and present themselves. That will enable them to neutralize the negative effects of emotional reaction to change and support people to make changes more easily.

Category: Teamwork

EI Feature: The emotional competency of emotional self-expression enables congruent communication.

EI Benefit: Team members can build trust and establish extraordinary rapport because with self-awareness and the ability to effectively express emotions they are able to be congruent - their words match their emotions and actions. People who are emotionally unaware often unconsciously act out their emotions and send mixed messages.

Category: Decision-Making

EI Feature: Emotional self-awareness enables people to recognize clearly which emotions are influencing their decisions and how.

EI Benefit: With emotional self-awareness people can be more clear and objective. The results are better decisions that are more readily supported by team members, fewer regrets, and more productive outcomes.

Your Turn

OK, now it's your turn. Consider what the problems are that your employees or clients want solutions to. How can emotional intelligence help solve those problems. Review the emotional skills and identify how they can be applied to get new and better results.

Express emotional intelligence in terms of features and benefits to help people recognize the value. And to really make an impact help them to experience both the problem and the benefit. Ask them, "If you can solve that problem, how would your life and work be different or better? How is that important to you?

To use features and benefits to get buy in and tap motivation, you need to:

Know

✓ What the problems are that your clients want and need solutions to.

✓ Which emotional skills will be required to solve the problem; and exactly how.

Have

✓ An interest in solving problems and not just promoting the subject of emotional intelligence.

✓ A basic understanding of the skills of EI.

Do

✓ Sell the sizzle and not the steak.

✓ Ask the client how the solution will make their life better.

Chapter 7: An EQ Development Plan

Unlike IQ, which is deemed to be fixed at one level for life, emotional intelligence or EQ can be infinitely developed. The elements of successful development include:

Motivation

As you know from your experience, to learn new skills you need motivation. Being motivated helps you overcome frustration and procrastination and stimulates you to practice.

Developing emotional intelligence requires strong motivation. To develop your EQ you must learn to effectively deal with your feelings, recognize and overcome self-limiting behaviors and adopt new ways of being.

> **To be most successful in developing your emotional skills, and the emotional skills of others, you will need to find ways to tap into intrinsic motivation - one's deeper purpose for making a positive change.**

Model

An emotional intelligence model helps people understand the skills they are developing and how those skills are related and relevant. With a model, learners can grasp the context of being emotionally intelligent and use the model as a guide for development. The most popular emotional intelligence model is Goleman's emotional competency model. There are other very useful models, including the EQ At Work Model.

As a facilitator of learning you need to understand the model that you are using and how best to use it. For example, Goleman's model represents workplace competencies based on emotional skills. As an EQ coach you must know what those underlying emotional skills are, how they affect workplace behaviors and what must be understood, experienced and practiced to learn them.

Method

If you decided to learn a foreign language you could choose from several methods. With one method you learn by memorizing the words. Another, method helps you learn by associating everyday objects with new words and phrases.

Proponents of the association learning method say that experiencing the new language in context is more fun than memorizing and much more successful. Developing emotional competence that lasts also requires something other than memorization. It is difficult, if not impossible, to embody emotional skills by only thinking or talking *about* them or by just reading a book or watching a movie – it takes *doing* them or having an experience.

For that reason, a half-day workshop in emotional intelligence is also not likely to produce lasting beneficial change of behavior. Change is a process, not an event. It requires a combination of experiencing the concepts, specific practice and support over time.

Example: The EQ At Work Method

Using my EQ At Work model as an example, a typical learning engagement might include all of the following and in this order:

1. **Introductory presentation:** A 45 - 90 minute experiential program that informs and engages participants and motivates them to take action to further develop their EQ.

2. **Assessment:** Rating either or both emotional and workplace competencies to increase client awareness and identify goals.

3. **Experiential Workshop:** 1/2 day to 3 days, to experience the concepts and establish common principles and practices for further development.

4. **EQ coaching:** Typically 8-12 weeks of weekly support sessions with a qualified EQ coach to develop and apply skills to real world situations. See Chapters 11 through 17 for more about EQ coaches.

5. **Practice:** Daily or weekly activities to develop emotional muscle and establish new behaviors.

6. **Follow-up support:** Coaching and or managerial support to reinforce the concepts for 6 or months

Practice

All my years of teaching emotional intelligence have been spent in working with adult learners. Two things I have noticed, that sabotage adult learners are:

1. They hold the belief that they "should know how to do this," and

2. They assume that change is too easy. They say, "oh, now that you have made me aware of what I am doing I will just do it differently."

There is no good reason why you "should know how to do this."

> **Up until now there has been little support or encouragement for emotional intelligence development from parents, schools, society and the workplace. In fact, it has been the opposite; we have been discouraged.**

The traditional workplace attitude of "leave your emotions at the door," is still prevalent.

One day, perhaps, we will reach a stage where emotional intelligence is a required standard subject in schools and universally recognized as an advantage in business. So no, you shouldn't be expected to know this and changing habits is too difficult with just a casual approach. It takes specific practice.

Let's use sports as an example. If you were a golfer who was consistently slicing your tee shot because of the habit of a crooked swing, a golf pro might tell you to practice by hitting balls at the driving range while holding your right arm firmly next to your body.

Changing your emotional habits is probably more difficult than changing a golf swing, but an EQ coach would also give you a specific behavioral practice to develop the skill of managing an emotional situation. One time it might be as simple as a mantra like saying to yourself: "this is not about me." Or it might be a way to express your feelings effectively.

Support

Coaching is the ideal support mechanism. A coach can teach new concepts, help you apply new skills and give you feedback to make corrections, Your coach will provide encouragement when you are struggling, acknowledge your progress, and help you turn your successful behaviors into new productive habits.

If you ask a client, "how would more emotional awareness be valuable to you, I promise you they will easily recognize that emotional awareness can be valuable to them in enabling better choices. But if you ask them how they will develop the skill of recognizing their emotions in the moment, they will probably be blank.

A trained EQ coach can help break the learning down into small bites and develop one part of the desired skill at a time. In each part of that learning process the coach gives the client small behavioral assignments or practices that develop the skill and each skill builds upon the previous.

Example: The EQ At Work Coaching Process

In each coaching session, an EQ At Work trained coach, supports the client to:

✓ **Develop and apply emotional skills** - EG. Recognizing and understanding emotions.

✓ **Develop and apply decision-making skills** - Using emotional awareness to inform decision-making.

✓ **Adopt behavioral practices** - Create and use skill-building practices

✓ **Create support** - Create and use structures and systems that support integration of new behaviors.

To prepare yourself to facilitate the development of emotional intelligence, you need to:

Know

✓ How to tap the intrinsic motivation of your clients/learners

✓ How to recognize and understand emotions.

✓ How to use emotions to inform decisions.

✓ How to create new habits.

Have

✓ A model that helps people understand and relate to what they are learning

✓ A structured method to follow which leads step-by-step to improvement

✓ Development practices for skill building

Do

✓ Practice using techniques to develop your own emotional skills so that from that experience you can credibly and effectively support others.

Chapter 8: What Didn't Work; What Did

The following two stories demonstrate what didn't work and what did, in implementing an emotional intelligence development initiative.

Rena's Story

Several years ago Rena, leader of the training team in her financial services organization, contacted me. She had been charged with the responsibility of implementing a leadership development program. Her top management wanted their leaders to build trust, create employee engagement to improve performance and inspire to staff to positive action.

"The lack of emotional intelligence is a real problem," she said. "The supervisors ride roughshod over the staff and people don't trust them anymore. People on the team don't feel acknowledged and are not engaged." "This is a very traditional firm," she went on, "they are resistant to that 'touchy feely' stuff and we are going to have be very cautious." "What I plan to do," she said, is to start very slowly with just an assessment and ramp up slowly to add training when they are not so resistant."

The slow ramp up approach Rena described sounds reasonable, but it failed, and Rena and her three-person team were subsequently fired. What went wrong?

Rena and her team decided that they shouldn't "ruffle any feathers." Instead of building trust, creating engagement and inspiring leaders, they were timid, apologetic, and as they described it, "politically correct" with the leaders they were training.

They never challenged the status quo. They asked for and expected little, from the leaders they were training. They were so deferential that they were dismissed by their leader clients as ineffective and unnecessary.

The approach of just using assessments worked against Rena and her team. She believed that emotional intelligence assessments alone would create such awareness and be so convincing, that leaders would see the need to develop greater emotional skill. This approach depended on leaders seeing EI as a good idea because it was logical., but it left out emotions. She and her team never tapped the leaders' intrinsic motivation and failed to inspire them to action. The large investment Rena made in providing assessments for each leader, which was seen as a useless expense by the company.

Rena did not have a next step planned either. In fact she had no plan except to react to whatever the leaders did. Neither she nor her staff, attempted to invite leaders to a workshop or a presentation to enroll them in EQ coaching. Her leader clients only did the assessment because they were told they had to.

To be successful what Rena really needed to

Know

✓ What was intrinsically motivating to her leader clients.

Have

✓ A complete plan and the courage to implement it.

Do

✓ Maintain her integrity and be authentically powerful instead of trying to just be politically correct.

✓ Learn ways to get people engaged and inspired.

Ginger's Story

Ginger was the lead trainer in a large insurance company. Her job was virtually identical to Rena's and she too had been charged with the responsibility of implementing a leadership development program. Her people also wanted leaders to build trust, create employee engagement to improve performance and inspire staff to positive action.

Ginger's approach was very different from Rena's. From the beginning she was non-apologetic and proactive. She took a leadership role and kept doing whatever she had to, to create success.

Ginger used the EQ At Work development plan, described in Chapter 7 with minor customization to suit her audience. The results were:

1. Successful development of approximately 120 leaders in the company.

2. Improved performance and teamwork.

3. Her promotion to head of training for her entire division, for which she credits her personal growth from administering the emotional intelligence development program, as well as the performance results participants achieved.

Here's what Ginger did to achieve success:

Introductory workshops

She started by inviting me to conduct an introductory workshop, held at her organization's main office, to get the first level of buy in. The presentation was very successful. Ginger then presented a series of similar events for employees.

Senior Management Support

Ginger was convinced that she needed the blessing and support of top level executives in her company but knew the well entrenched "dinosaurs," as they were referred to by some employees, were unlikely to volunteer to participate in the EQ coaching and training with the rest of the leaders. So, she worked with me to design a half-day orientation program just for them. She delivered the program and those senior executives were provided with tools and strategies for supporting the success of the emotional intelligence initiative. And they did!

Simple Assessment

Instead of making an investment in a validated assessment Ginger used a simple one-page emotional intelligence questionnaire to build initial awareness and begin the training and coaching dialogue.

In Ginger's case, her organization had previously provided 360 degree feedback assessments to the leadership team, with a focus on leadership competency. Her interest was to not overwhelm leaders with yet another assessment, but instead keep the EQ assessment simple. She wanted to get the EQ conversation started first and the simple questionnaire helped her do that.

An Experiential Workshop

Ginger then conducted multiple 3-day EQ leadership training programs, for groups of 20 leaders, using the EQ At Work model. The workshops landed the major concepts, and created shared vocabulary and meaning through shared experience.

2 Months of Coaching

Next she followed with two months of EQ group coaching, with groups of four people, to support leaders to develop skill and apply it on the job.

> **"The results are awesome," she reported. Not only are employees more engaged and performing better, but the coaching groups became social groups. These same people are getting together after hours for a few beers and some laughs. The camaraderie is extraordinary."**

Ginger reported that leadership influence; teamwork and collaboration were improved among this group.

What enabled Ginger's success was that she:

Knew

✓ What really motivated her audience.

Had

✓ Courage, commitment and a plan.

Did

✓ Whatever she needed to do to be successful.

Learn more about introductory workshops in Chapter 10.

Chapter 9: About Emotional Intelligence Assessments

What are they? What do they measure? How are they used? Should you use them or not?

Assessments are typically used in coaching and training to evaluate development needs, identify strengths and opportunities for growth, set goals and monitor progress. A wide variety of assessment tools are available to evaluate almost anything including such things as personality characteristics, workplace skills, decision-making ability, learning styles and leadership ability. *And yes, there are assessments to measure emotional intelligence but before using them it is important for you to understand what they measure and how.*

In my 15 years of practice I have used many different EI assessments in working with clients including all the major assessments and those of my own design. My company EQ At Work was also a distributor and national training center for three years for Genos EI, a major EI assessment provider.

> **My purpose here is not to provide an in-depth description or analysis of all EQ assessments but to make you aware of how assessments are different, to share my insights and experience about the use of assessments and to help you understand your choices.**

Three Major Types

Most people are familiar with personality assessments and assume that EI assessments determine scores in a similar way but that is not completely true. As there are different models of emotional intelligence there are different types of EI assessments. If you plan to use an EI assessment, get clear on what is measured and how. Read the material and take a sample assessment before you commit. The three most used types of EI assessments measure emotional intelligence based on abilities, traits or competencies.

1. **Abilities-based:** The MSCEIT emotional intelligence assessment created by Mayer, Salovey and Caruso from their emotional intelligence model *measures EI based on one's ability to perform certain emotional tasks*. It is well researched and powerful. My clients found it intimidating and complex and said it was like a "psychological test."

2. **Trait-based:** The EQi, created by Reuven Bar-On was the first attempt to define and quantify emotional quotient. EQi *measures EI based on traits deemed necessary to successfully cope with one's environment.* I appreciate the whole person approach and the instrument is well researched and validated. My business clients sometimes commented that the language seemed more personal than business and had difficulty relating it to the workplace. My complaint with all trait-based tools, including all the social styles assessments, is that they tend to get misused. The measures are frequently used to label and pigeonhole people. I hear people say things like "Oh you are a high D, or ENFP or whatever, and that's why you do that."

3. **Competency-based:** The EI 360 is based on Daniel Goleman's emotional competency model, explained in Chapter 2 on emotional intelligence, and was the first multi-rater assessment. *The EI 360 measures emotional competencies that enhance workplace performance.* I prefer competency-type assessments because you can easily transfer assessment results to coaching and training. They enable you to identify desired workplace behaviors, and then develop the skills needed to create those behaviors. With competencies, you can evaluate progress through observation. I also find multi-rater assessments to provide more valuable information. See my comments below. Visit http://www.eiconsortium.org/measures/eci_360.html for more details on the Goleman EI 360.

Social Styles Assessments: A number of providers of personality profiles or social styles instruments have repositioned them as emotional intelligence assessments. These assessments do not quantify emotional intelligence but relate one's social style or behavior preferences with interpersonal and interpersonal skill. Many years ago I used personality profiles to increase people's awareness and to begin training programs in communication and teamwork. I have not used them in connection with emotional intelligence training.

What is a validated assessment?

Simply put, validation is a scientific process of testing the questions and structure of an assessment with controlled groups of users. The primary purpose is to refine a set of questions that create a stable measuring tool that delivers consistent, predictable results. Validated assessments are regarded as more credible and reliable because of this testing.

Be clear that any type of assessment can be validated. I once had a trainer tell me that he chose a particular EI assessment to work with because it "is the most validated one out there," but he didn't really understand what was being measured and how it was relevant.

Self-Assessment and Multi-rater Assessments

Self-Assessments

A self-assessment relies on the client's ability to be objective and truthful, which is particularly difficult with emotional skills, and I think, limits their usefulness.

As well intentioned as people are, they typically tend to overstate their ability. Or, they answer questions in ways they think they should rather than be bluntly honest with themselves. No matter how well constructed self-assessments are, they are prone to this limitation. Self-assessments can, however, still be useful in increasing awareness and creating a starting point for a coaching conversation.

Multi-Rater Assessments

Multi-rater or 360 degree assessments are those in which a client rates herself and is also rated on the same questions by multiple raters who typically include manager, peers, direct reports and clients.

It is often the difference between how someone rated himself or herself versus how they were rated by others that makes them so useful. I prefer competency-based, multi-rater assessments, like the EI 360, because they reflect back to the subject how others perceive their behavior and what real opportunities they have for improving performance and workplace relationship.

> **Used properly, multi-rater assessments, also called 360-degree assessments, can provide motivation and possibility for people who have been blind to how they are behaving and how their behavior affects others.**

Assessment Certification

Most validated assessments require a coach or trainer to qualify to use them by attending special training. The training is typically done in a weekend workshop and average costs are around $2500 plus travel expenses. You should consider this investment carefully and ask yourself what you want to measure, how you will use the assessments and how often. You might decide that it makes more sense for you to invest in coach training. There are several good coach certification programs, The EQ At Work program among them, which provide 6 months of training for a cost similar to a weekend assessment certification.

Should you buy an EI assessment, use your own or use none at all?

The answer to that question depends on your intention. Do you want to inform or transform? Do you just want to try to create interest or are you working toward lasting change? Some trainers use an emotional intelligence assessment and a feedback session as their only improvement process.

> **Many believe that simply using an assessment to make people more aware and suggesting new behaviors is sufficient to produce a beneficial change. In my experience that is an expensive "band-aid" approach**

that is not likely to produce meaningful or lasting benefit.

I use some form of assessment with every client. With some, especially recalcitrant clients, a 360-degree EI assessment can provide the jolt of reality that opens them to change.

With other clients, especially the highly motivated, a simple EI questionnaire that stimulates their thinking and encourages them to do some self-examination is sufficient to start the coaching dialogue or initiate a training program.

More and more companies report using their own 360 competency assessments, instead of EI assessments, to set goals and measure progress. That can be a smart approach and reduce costs if you define the competency you want, then identify and develop the underlying emotional skills required through coaching and training.

I am sure assessment providers would prefer that their assessment be provided to every employee as a part of every EI coaching and training engagement. And some might assert that using their assessment will improve training results. I don't find that to absolutely be the case. And especially when resources are limited, and you need to get the biggest bang for the buck, you may want to consider other options.

Which choice will get you the biggest bang for the buck?

Recently I observed a case in which an organization retained a consultant to provide multi-rater emotional intelligence assessments and a feedback coaching session to each of 75 leaders. Then the 12 lowest scoring leaders were provided 3 months of EQ development coaching. The total investment was about $90,000. Would this company have gotten better performance results using that investment to just provide EQ coaching for 30 leaders? I think so.

Consider Ginger's story in Chapter 8. Ginger trained 120 leaders for far less than $90,000 by sending two people to coaching school to become internal EQ coaches and by using a simple low cost questionnaire. See the EQ At Work Questionnaire in the Appendix for an example of what you might acquire or create.

About assessments - what you need to:

Know

- ✓ What the purpose of your assessment is.

- ✓ What your assessment is measuring.

- ✓ How you will transfer the assessment to learning.

Have

- ✓ A clear understanding of the workplace competencies you want to improve and how emotional intelligence supports them.

Do

- ✓ Be clear idea on what your approach to training and coaching will be and the role of assessments within it.

- ✓ Choose an assessment technique and tools that best help you accomplish learning objectives.

Chapter 10: The Introductory Presentation

An introductory presentation or short workshop is a great way to attract internal clients, create acceptance for an EQ development program and enroll people in EQ coaching and training. Your chances of getting your ideas across and having them received are increased when you demonstrate some of the skills of an emotionally intelligent facilitator by creating an environment in which:

- ✓ Learners are engaged
- ✓ Participation is vigorous
- ✓ Ideas land in both head and heart
- ✓ People are motivated
- ✓ The "Aha moment" is experienced:

Here are 6 high EQ ideas to help you create an engaging experience that stimulates, satisfies and enrolls.

Less Is More

I often talk with coaches and trainers who are planning a speech or a workshop and want ideas to help make it effective. Almost always, their plan is to load up the program with content. They support this approach by telling themselves things like: "More information is better because it makes me look more knowledgeable, people really want more information and facts are convincing." In this more is better approach, I have seen them prepare a 30-slide presentation for a 45 minute talk.

Stop. I understand that you want to do a great job, but overloading your program with content and focusing on facts could put you at risk of failing.

Usually the reason that we think we need more is that we are anxious about our ability to be perceived as valuable. We are scared that we can't stand up and facilitate a learning experience without tons of details to prove our worth. It is simply not true.

Your ability to be present is what creates value... and that is the first lesson in emotionally intelligent presentation.

It's Not About You!

When you are anxious about performing it is easy to get stuck in making the presentation all about you. Thoughts like: "Do they like me?" and "Am I pleasing them," become more important than truly serving people and being a master of ceremonies of the learning experience.

Recognize and manage your emotions so that you can be present to the needs of your audience. Don't fake it. Stop and examine your feelings and put a name to them. If you are, tell yourself "I'm really anxious about doing this." And then do it anyway.

In some situations it is OK to share your feelings with your audience as a well of becoming more present but it must be done in a way that does not oblige them to take care of you in any way.

Make your training or presentation all about them!

Head and Heart

To be optimally effective you need to reach both the minds and hearts of your audience. I have observed presenters new to emotional intelligence trying to convince their audience of the value of EI with facts and bottom line proof. They believe that resistance can be overcome with logic alone. That simply is not true. Why do successful companies spend millions in advertising campaigns designed to tap into people's emotions?

Any sales professional will tell you, people make their choices more on emotion than logic.

Left Brain Food

Yes, it is very smart to give your audience some food for the left brain - facts and logic to help quiet their mind and satisfy their need to know. There is plenty of convincing arguments and proof of performance available from case studies. You can find good examples at:

http://eiconsortium.org/reports/business_case_for_ei.html

The Sanofi-Aventis Case Study Example

Here's an example of some convincing information from a study conducted by Genos Pty Ltd, the providers of the Genos EI assessment:

Sanofi-Aventis provided 40 sales managers with a six-month emotional intelligence development program of training and coaching. Actual sales results for sales reps that had undergone EI development were 13% higher than the results for the control group. Retention levels of key sales employees improved during and after the completion of the program. The program returned approximately 5 dollars for every 1 dollar the company invested during the 6-month period. (Genos 2007 http://www.genosinternational.com/)

> **Go ahead, use some facts to support your case, do so sparingly and provide more later if needed, but please, if you want to be truly effective, you must evoke experience.**

Experience Is Everything

You can tell me as many times as you like but until I experience what it is you are presenting, I do not really get it. You can vividly describe the taste of chocolate, but only a taste will create understanding. Experiences engender emotion, which creates learning. The late Paul MacLean, creator of the Triune brain theory said, as best as I can paraphrase,

"Without emotion there is no memory and without memory there is no learning."

> **Include one or two activities that evoke emotion and use that emotional experience to stimulate insight and tap into intrinsic motivation.**

If you want to save time, and start with something that works, a customizable introductory EQ presentation is available affordably at http://www.eqatwork.com

Start With The End In Mind

If all you want is to promote interest and provide an entertaining experience your job is done, but if you want more, you could use your introductory talk as an enrollment or selection process for further training.

> **Be ready to announce the next step in your plan and take advantage of the energy of your presentation to accelerate your progress.**

About introductory workshops, what you need to:

Know

- ✓ Less is more. Keep it simple.
- ✓ You need a combination of logic and emotion in your presentation.
- ✓ People do not choose on logic but on emotion.

Have

- ✓ A design that provides one or two emotional experiences.

Do

- ✓ Be open, flexible and present. Make the presentation about them and not about you.

Chapter 11: What Is An EQ Coach?

What is coaching?

Coaching is generally described as a method of guiding, instructing, and encouraging a person or group of people, with the aim to achieve some goal or develop and apply specific skills. A coach gives honest feedback and support, inspires, challenges, facilitates growth and change, and partners with the client to achieve stated goals.

Coaching as a profession has grown rapidly since about 1995 and gained wide acceptance in business as a method for improving performance. Today there are many types of business and personal coaching to help people be more successful. A wide variety of coaching specialties provides support for things like career, parenting, running an Internet business, writing a book or being a better leader and more.

Who are coaches and what makes them choose to coach?

Talk to coaches and those who want to be, and they will probably tell you something like, "I love to help people and I have been doing it most of my life. People are always asking me for support." Coaches are people that like to help and are always interested in learning and growing. HR professionals, trainers and consultants often become coaches as do school counselors and mental health professionals.

Organizations sometimes select leaders, managers or team members to be internal coaches. Some internal coaches act more as a mentor, sharing experience and expertise, and some are chosen to coach the development of emotional intelligence.

> Many believe that anyone can coach and I tend to agree - as long as they are willing to serve, willing to learn how to effectively support people, and are committed to their own growth.

What is different about emotional intelligence coaching?

> Emotional intelligence coaching is focused specifically on recognizing and using emotions to improve one's ability to manage one's own thoughts, feelings and actions, and one's ability to understand, relate with and positively influence others.

The goals of emotional intelligence coaching may include, reducing stress, increasing personal effectiveness, improving communication, managing conflict and change, increasing leadership influence and improving teamwork and collaboration.

The EQ Coach

An EQ Coach is both a teacher and a coach. EQ coaches teach clients the principles of emotional intelligence. Then the EQ coach guides and supports the client to develop emotional skills and apply them in real life situations to improve personal and interpersonal effectiveness and quality of life.

What training do coaches need?

> To be effective a coach needs to know how to build trust, ask good questions, listen and truly understand, and how to support people to take positive action.

If you are selecting employees to be internal coaches, evaluate them on the basis of these abilities and then get them training in emotional intelligence coaching, or retain certified EQ coaches. There are many successful coaches who have never had formal coach training, but most career coaches and successful internal coaches attend coaching school to develop advanced skills and become accredited.

I think that when you agree to be someone's coach, you take on an important responsibility that deserves the best you can give.

Coach training will teach you things you don't know and help you leverage the things you do, so that you are able to truly empower others.

What training do emotional intelligence coaches need?

Some people regard emotional intelligence as simply practicing the golden rule and being nice to people. Treating people with kindness and consideration is a part of the mix, but In fact, there is an art and science to emotional intelligence that goes beyond that.

While the subject need not intimidate you, effective EQ coaching requires some specialized knowledge and competency. To be an extraordinarily effective EQ coach you need to learn the same skills that are taught in traditional coaching schools, plus learn emotional skills. Read more about what those skills are in the next chapters.

About EQ coaching - what you need to:

Know

- ✓ The role and responsibilities of a coach.
- ✓ What's different about EQ coaching.
- ✓ How to build trust.
- ✓ How to ask good questions.
- ✓ How to listen and really hear what is meant.
- ✓ How to guide people to positive action.

Have

- ✓ Acceptance, patience and compassion.

✓ Basic command of essential coach competencies including building trust, asking good questions, listening and supporting clients to take positive action.

✓ The willingness to lead.

✓ The ability to demonstrate emotional intelligence.

Do

✓ Develop the unique skills of coaching emotional intelligence.

✓ Hire, or train with, an experienced EQ coach.

Chapter 12: Required Coach Competencies

What are the skills you need to effectively coach emotional intelligence?

To be an effective coach you need skills that are universally regarded by experienced professional coaches as essential to successful coaching. These skills are a part of the curriculum at most coaching schools and common to the certification requirements of The International Coach Federation (ICF) and The International Association of Coaching (IAC) for coach accreditation.

> **How would you rate your present ability in the following essential coaching skills?**

Effective Coaches:

- ✓ **Build trust:** Create an open and honest coaching relationship and a safe environment for learning and change.

- ✓ **Encourage and Inspire:** Recognize and acknowledge the client's ability, accomplishment and potential

- ✓ **Listen deeply:** Hear and understand the underlying meanings as well as what is said, and acknowledge and validate the client's experience.

- ✓ **Clarify:** Ask good questions that enable insight and discovery

- ✓ **Communicate:** Establish rapport that enables understanding and express yourself clearly and directly

✓ **Empower accountability:** Support the client to keep their commitments to themselves and work towards intended outcomes

✓ **Co-create support systems and environments:** Help the client identify and create relationships and structures that support success.

Emotional Skills

Additionally, emotional intelligence coaches need to develop the core emotional skills discussed in Chapter 3, and essential emotional intelligence coaching competencies, to support clients to success.

I have created online assessments to help you rate your present ability in these essential personal and professional emotional intelligence skills. *Please see the Appendix.* I list them here for reference.

Personal EQ Skills: The EQ At Work Core Skills Questionnaire

Emotional Self-awareness:

1. I can sense and name my emotions, in the moment.

2. I can experience my emotions and accept them and myself without judgment.

Self-Management

3. I take responsibility for my emotional experience.

4. I use my emotions as information for effective decision-making.

5. I manage my emotions to maintain a positive attitude.

6. I respond to strongly emotionally stimulating situations effectively instead of reacting impulsively.

Social Awareness

7. I can sense and name the emotions of others, in the moment.

8. I use my emotional awareness to gain insight into others' needs and concerns.

Relationship Management

9. I effectively express my emotions to communicate successfully.

10. I effectively manage and positively influence the emotions of others.

Professional EQ skills:

1. Create extraordinary rapport.

2. Motivate and influence clients to become engaged in, and take responsibility for, their learning and change.

3. Teach clients to perceive, understand, manage, express and use emotions to better manage themselves and relate with and influence others.

4. Evoke and use emotional experience to enable deep self-insight and self-understanding.

5. Create specific behavioral practices for clients that develop emotional skills.

About coach competency - what you need to:

Know

✓ How to recognize the universally accepted coach competencies of: building trust, asking good questions and listening and supporting clients to take positive action.

✓ Which of these competencies are your strengths now.

✓ Which coaching competencies you need to develop.

Have

✓ Willingness to learn and practice

✓ Confidence that you can and will be an effective EQ coach.

✓ Basic ability in the core emotional skills of self-awareness, self-management, social awareness and relationship management.

✓ Basic ability to demonstrate EQ coaching skills including building rapport, tapping intrinsic motivation, teaching core emotional skills and helping clients craft specific behavior practices.

Do

✓ Develop your own emotional intelligence.

✓ Develop basic command of each coaching competency

Chapter 13: The EQ Coaching Process

What are the steps to coaching emotional intelligence?

The process of coaching emotional intelligence includes many of the elements previously described in this book. Here's my recommendation for a step-by-step approach.

Begin with preparing yourself to coach.

Whether you have had coach training or not, you will benefit by study and practice of the coaching competencies described in Chapter 12. Pay attention and observe those skills being used by yourself and others. For example, focus on the coaching competency of building trust. Notice how others develop trust with you. What made that trust possible? What did they say and do?

You can practice many of the coach competencies, like building trust, listening deeply, asking good questions that clarify, and encouraging and inspiring others in your day to day work and life without being in a formal coaching situation. Focus your attention on one competency at a time.

Develop your own emotional intelligence.

Commit now to the study and practice of the core emotional skills. Again, focus your attention on one skill at a time. For example, what can you do to be better able to recognize emotions? What stops you from being more aware? What supports you to be more aware? What steps will you take?

As with the coach competencies, you can practice EQ skills as you move through life every day. Practice with you and the people you come in contact with - even the waitperson who serves you lunch, your neighbor or your family members. Even if you never become an EQ coach, you will enjoy life more.

Introduce and get buy in.

Introduce the concept of emotional intelligence both intellectually and experientially. Be able to describe features and benefits. See Chapter 6 to get a jump start.

Tap intrinsic motivation.

Begin up front to conquer the natural internal resistance to change by helping people find their deepest motivation. How is the development of these skills going to change things? How will their life and work be different and better? Find what is really important to them and help them remember that's what they want.

Make clear agreements with clients.

When you are ready to start coaching, start off with clear agreements with each client. How will they define success? How will you *be* together? What rules and conditions will you have?

Create a safe, creative environment for learning.

Make it easier to learn emotional skills by creating a safe, predictable context for learning. Part of creating such a context is in making clear agreements so the client knows what to expect. Part of creating that context is how you are being. Be accepting, patient, non-judgmental, equal and supportive...and as emotionally intelligent as you can be.

Follow a coaching plan.

Decide on how many sessions of coaching are included in your plan and what you will accomplish. How often will you meet, and, for how long?

You should be able to tell the client what they are going to learn and how that will happen. For example: My EQ At Work basic coaching plan is for weekly sessions of 45 minutes for each of 12 weeks.

Use a model.

If you don't create your own model or use another, like the EQ At Work Model, Goleman's model is a good frame of reference to help people understand the concepts, and guide development.

Start with core skills.

As a coach, my preference is to teach the core emotional skills and empower people by helping them to develop those abilities first. Then after they have a basic grasp of those skills, I support them to apply those skills to life and work situations.

Chunk it down.

Break the learning down into bite size chunks that can be easily digested by the learner. For example, what are the components of empathy? Is acceptance one of them? How do you develop acceptance? How do you remove the barriers? How do you practice acceptance?

Give them a practice.

Talking about emotional skills is one thing, but it is practicing them that creates new behaviors. Craft specific practice assignments that build skills. And also create assignments that apply the skills in real life situations.

Acknowledge their progress and go for more.

Celebrate each learning success by acknowledging the client for what they have accomplished and having them acknowledge themselves. Then, invite the client to go for more with the next level of development.

Get Advanced Training

The outline above gives you a solid approach to create a successful coaching engagement. What you may want more of are specific methods for teaching and coaching. You may want to know what to put in a lesson plan or what questions to ask when coaching. Or you may want to know what techniques to use to develop emotional skills.

> **If your intention is to be as effective as possible in producing lasting behavioral change, I recommend that you get advanced training. You will accelerate your progress; you won't have to reinvent the wheel. And, you will gain proven tools and techniques.**

For example, in my EQ Coach and Trainer Certification you would learn a specific method for teaching each emotional skill. You would command a coaching model that includes specific questions to ask that lead the client from insight to action. There's 20 years of experience and information packed into that course. More than enough to fill another book - which is in process now.

To effectively coach emotional intelligence, what you need to:

Know

- ✓ How to create safe, creative learning environments.
- ✓ How to get buy in and tap intrinsic motivation.
- ✓ How to create a coaching plan.
- ✓ How to chunk the learning into small bites.
- ✓ How to create practices.

Have

- ✓ Basic coaching competencies.
- ✓ Basic EQ competencies.

✓ A coaching plan.

✓ Methods and activities for teaching emotional skills.

Do

✓ Prepare yourself to coach.

✓ Make clear agreements for coaching.

✓ Follow a coaching plan.

✓ Acknowledge progress.

Chapter 14: Who To Coach; Who Not

Not all people who "need" coaching are good coaching prospects.

Perhaps you have considered where to get started with coaching in your organization and have thought, "Now she really needs emotional intelligence coaching." I understand. Based on your observation of someone's behavior you might see where an improvement in their social skills would make them more effective and easier to work with. But does that make them a good candidate for EQ coaching? Maybe, or maybe not. It depends on their motivation and readiness.

Clients need motivation to be coachable.

Motivation is necessary for success in any learning or change. It is even more important when learning to recognize and manage emotions. Long ago, after some vivid learning experiences, I made the choice to only coach motivated clients. When clients are motivated they are coachable - open to new information, trusting, willing to be vulnerable, and responsible in completing assignments and practices. If you don't have those things in the EQ coaching relationship, you are unlikely to see any positive results.

The Pain, Gain or Complain Clients

There was a time when I did a lot of executive EQ coaching with clients who had been referred to me by their company. I associated them with one of three categories of motivation labeled the "pain, gain or complain" clients.

"Pain" clients were experiencing the pain of ineffective behaviors and poor interpersonal skills. They may have been put on notice by their company to change or else. They were not simply motivated by fear of job loss. They liked their work; they were good at it and had valuable experience. They truly wanted to make a contribution and it was painful to them that their lack of EQ skills was preventing them from doing so. They made excellent coaching clients.

The second category was the "gain" clients. They had decided that they wanted to play a bigger game - to be more and do more in their organization and in their world. These folks were ones who had made a realistic assessment of their abilities and decided that in order to achieve their goals they must increase their emotional competency. They were superb clients and typically made the greatest gains.

And finally there were the "complain" people. These were people who only showed up for the evaluation appointment because they were told to. They were not ready or able to see their part in the results they were getting. They thought they were victims and blamed their manager or their company for the problems they were having. Very few of these "complain" candidates ever benefited from coaching. I was able to make a connection with some and they got some good results, but for the most part, I had to go back to their company and advise that they were not good coaching candidates at this time.

> **Trying to force coaching upon those who are not ready or willing is disrespectful and abusive. It is better to wait until they come around or perhaps take other management action.**

There's a coaching rule I teach my students: "Don't go where you are not invited." In a productive coaching relationship a mutual invitation and acceptance is in place that creates trust and possibility. *If you don't have an invitation, don't coach.*

Using Assessments To Choose Coaching Candidates

Some consultants and companies attempt to choose coaching candidates using only assessment results. A common approach is to provide an EI assessment to a group. – Perhaps all the leaders or members of a team. Then EQ coaching is provided to those who scored lowest overall on the assessment. The intention is to increase overall team performance by only coaching the individuals in this low scoring group. That approach is not likely to be wholly effective. For, as I have said before, motivation and willingness is required on the part of each coaching candidate.

A Different Approach

A different approach has more potential - open the coaching to anyone on the team who is motivated, regardless of his or her assessment score. Starting with the most motivated spread the influence of emotional intelligence like a virus. Those motivated learners will more quickly express emotional intelligence in their behaviors. Emotional intelligence is infectious. The more you give it the more you have. Recruit those early adopters to help spread the word.

People who are giving (using or demonstrating) emotional intelligence will influence others to want it. For example: When people have greater emotional self awareness they make better choices and get better results. Other people who are not yet receiving coaching will notice and want similar success. Then they will be looking for EQ development for themselves. Self-aware people, knowing how their emotions are influencing their behavior, are also more resourceful. That enables them to deal with change and conflict and more effectively. This too will be noticed and coveted by others who will open up to you for coaching.

> **When people are more aware of others' emotions, they are more sensitive to those people's need and concerns. This sensitivity and empathy positively influences the behavior and effectiveness of those who are receiving. They now are more likely to treat others with sensitivity and empathy.**

When people are using the emotional skill of listening, those who are heard tend to trust more and trust creates improved relationship. The experience of greater trust and improved relationships will also convince more people to develop their EQ because they have an experience of the value.

Coaching The Supervisors

Here's another element to consider when deciding who and how to coach - coaching the supervisor. I have an associate in Mexico City who has a simple rule for coaching agreements: He insists on coaching the supervisor of any employee that is referred to him for coaching. There is much merit in this approach. The relationship between the supervisor and the employee is very influential.

A supervisor who is using emotional intelligence will be a positive influence in the development of emotional intelligence of one of her direct reports.

> **A supervisor who is not involved and not specifically supportive of the coaching may, and often does, undermine the learning and limit the coaching results. For top results, coach the supervisor of the people you are coaching.**

About who to coach - what you need to:

Know

- ✓ Not everyone is coachable… today.
- ✓ Coaching, and especially EQ coaching, requires a motivated client.
- ✓ You will be more successful when you coach the supervisor of the people you are trying to develop.

Have

- ✓ A willing, coachable client.

Do

- ✓ Start with those who are most motivated and spread EQ like a virus.
- ✓ For top results coach the supervisor of the people you are coaching.

Chapter 15: But, Will They Like It?

When I conduct webinars for coaches and trainers interested in developing emotional intelligence, these kinds of questions always come up: "I'm working with some pretty traditional people. Are you sure they are going to like this?" Or, "The leaders I am being asked to train are not open to anything emotional. How are they going to accept EQ?"

I have had much experience developing leadership EQ and among my clients were many hard-core traditional, non-emotional, conservative leaders. I worked with leaders and managers in all kinds or organizations including hi-tech firms, government agencies and financial firms that were all thought of as being especially conservative. At first there were times I doubted myself, and them, and wondered, "Are they going to accept these ideas? Will they do the learning activities? Can I get them to open up and be self-disclosing and vulnerable?" And, "Are they going to like it?" Based on my experience, what I can tell you is...

They are going to love it!

I was always touched by how the people, especially the men, in the leadership emotional intelligence programs I conducted, opened up. Once they got a taste of what was possible they took to it like a duck to water. And they learned and they changed, sometimes remarkably.

> **My experience with learners continues to confirm my belief that all humans have a longing for emotional and spiritual connection with themselves and others.**

When people are in an environment where emotional connection with themselves and others is accepted and possible, and offered a chance to connect, they do.

It is heartwarming to see people come into my workshops or into coaching, initially being wary and defensive and cool, and then show their sensitivity and caring. So will they like it? Absolutely.

They are going to love it!

All of them? No, not every one. Some people are just not ready to connect with themselves, and their emotions, when you are ready to teach. It might be as many as one third of the group you are assigned to work with. As I mentioned in Chapter 14: Who To Coach; Who Not, **"Don't go where you are not invited."** This is not the time to persuade or to force. It is a time for understanding, acceptance, compassion and patience. Meet them where they are. Give them what they are ready for. And then, give them time and many of them will come around. And some may not be ready until their next lifetime.

They will love it If you:

Know

   ✓ How to create a safe, inviting and emotionally intelligent learning environment.

Have

   ✓ Faith in the human desire for connection.

   ✓ Courage and confidence.

Do

   ✓ Stay present and connected.

   ✓ Accept everyone, without judgment, as they are right now.

   ✓ Demonstrate by being, what you are asking them to do.

   ✓ Be a leader.

Chapter 16: Group Coaching

In the mid 1980's when I started coaching small groups, "group coaching" was virtually unheard of. Today a Google search for that term will yield you over 13 million pages. You will find specialty coaching groups on many subjects including leadership, Internet marketing, getting a job or writing a blog. And there are many advertisements for tools and instruction for running a group. Why all the interest and activity? Because group coaching works.

I started coaching small groups as part of a six-month training intensive. My training partner and I recognized that our participants learned faster and remembered more when they got specific individual support. We did not have the resources to provide one-on-one coaching to these folks so we formed groups of four people and created a format that supported them.

> **Group coaching is appealing to participants because it offers, a sense of community, the opportunity to learn from the experiences of others, the opportunity for some individual attention and a lower cost than individual coaching.**

Organizations like group coaching as a part of the development mix, as it provides and opportunity to develop more people at a lower cost. In developing an organization or team, you might create a plan that includes participation in a workshop for everyone, individual coaching for leaders, and group coaching for staff.

Group coaching is good for independent coaches because it increases their hourly rate, builds a community of clients who are prospects for individual coaching, and gives them an attractive lower price alternative to market.

Group coaching is similar to individual coaching in purpose and method. Members with similar goals meet two to four times a month for learning and support. Coaches provide lessons and individual coaching and feedback as part of the process.

How do you run an effective group coaching program?

Group coaching works best when you have a structure and a process.

You want your group to be safe and inviting and an effective environment for learning, and so do your clients. Provide that environment by giving them a consistent format and meeting flow; a lesson plan for each meeting; effective facilitation and your leadership.

Intact Work Groups

Group coaching sometimes works well with intact work groups, and other times not. It depends on the level of commitment and trust. With trust, an intact team can actually progress faster. They gain a common language and share common principles and practices that enable them to better support each other.

I have had some groups where the supervisor is part of the group and if that person can be transparent and equal, not just during the meetings but in day to day contact, they group can thrive and become a more effective team. When there is fear in the team, group coaching effectiveness diminishes because people are not willing to be self-disclosing.

About group coaching - what you need to:

Know

- ✓ Coaching a group requires the same skills as individual coaching and the willingness to lead.
- ✓ Group dynamics aid the learning process.

✓ People learn by listening as well as by being coached.

Have

✓ Norms and rules for your group that create trust. EG the agreement to "keep confidential" everything that takes place in the group.

✓ A consistent format for the conduct of sessions.

✓ A lesson plan for each meeting.

Do

✓ Take a leadership role in facilitating your group.

✓ Develop emotional intelligence skills of group facilitation that enable you to - maintain your presence and composure, create safety, stimulate participation.

✓ Make the group experience engaging and worthwhile.

Chapter 17: The Influential Difference

Once your student sits down in your classroom, what will make the greatest difference in how much she will learn? Once the coaching conversation begins with your client, what will have the greatest influence on his progress?

You! You are the influential difference in learning, change and growth. That is true about the facilitator of any subject, and it is especially true in the development of emotional intelligence.

To understand your influence consider that two elements that are involved in determining your results, when you conduct coaching or training, are:

✓ What you do, and

✓ *How you are being* when you do it.

What you do is important because that provides necessary support for you and your clients or learners. Presenting the right information, in the right sequence, with the right materials are examples of things that are important for you to do to get good results.

How you are being when you do those things makes all the difference. Your way of being, the nature and quality of your behavior, has the single greatest influence on outcomes in your training and your coaching. Nothing that you can do will be more powerful than that. So how must you be to most positively influence learning?

Three ways you must be to most powerfully influence learning outcomes are:

1. Be present

2. Be connected

3. Be contextual

Be Present

What does being present mean to you?

When I have asked that question of my students they respond with things like "being in the moment" or "being in the now." Let's agree for this conversation that being present is being mentally, physically and emotionally focused on each moment. To be present, you have to be here in his moment - not in the past or future but right now. So that means you cannot be focused on the future as when you are thinking, "oh my goodness, what do I do next? You cannot be focused on the past, as when you are still caught up in the thoughts and feelings of a disagreement you had just before class or your coaching session started. You cannot be focused on other problems, deadlines or whatever.

> **Now those things sound obvious. What's not so obvious, and frequently happens unconsciously, is losing your focus on the present, because you are caught up in an emotional agenda.**

For example, it's possible to have an emotional agenda around being approved of. Fear, perhaps of being rejected, has you focused on getting people to like you rather than being focused on being present to the needs of your audience and being effective.

What is important about being present?

When you are present you can tune in acutely to your client or audience, you can really hear the meaning behind the words they say. You can respond instead of reacting, choosing the most appropriate and effective things to say and do. Being present, moment-to-moment is easier said than done. What enables one to be present?

What are the skills that enable one to focus on this moment? Interestingly, they are skills of emotional intelligence.

If you are emotionally self-aware that means that you are tuned in to you - you are recognizing the emotions that are influencing your thoughts and actions. If you are also effective at emotional self-management, you can be fully available to your clients or students. You must be tuned in, and connected to, you first, in order to be tuned in to, and make full connection with somebody else. If you are aware of what your emotions are and are able to manage yourself by being a compassionate witness to your emotions, but not have them dictate your behavior, you can be fully present.

For example, you may feel anxious and think "I must perform," so that people will approve of you. Or, you may think, "I hope I'm doing this right." To experience the feeling of anxiety, to sense and acknowledge your feeling and to be able to stay in the moment, is what's required to be present. So, your emotional skills, including emotional self-awareness, and emotional self-management are critical to staying present.

What disables being in the present is denial or avoidance of your emotions. For example, you may have had thoughts like this: "I am anxious about this presentation today. But I've been told to leave my emotions at home and put them behind me and I'm not going to pay any attention to that fear. I'm not really afraid anyway. That's nonsense that fear stuff. Come on, I'm able to get past that." That's how we were trained by our society and our workplaces to think and act, but it doesn't work.

What does work is to witness the emotion, to acknowledge the emotion and to regulate or command the emotions instead of having it command you. That doesn't mean denial or avoidance. That means staying present to your experience. And the degree to which you can stay present to your experience is communicated to your audience whether that audience is one or a thousand.

That demonstration of being present teaches very powerfully. You are providing your client or audience the vicarious experience of being emotionally aware,

self-managing and present. There's no other way to equal that level of power in teaching.

Be Connected

To be connected is to be in a relationship of extraordinary rapport with your client or audience. It is that extraordinary rapport that creates trust and engagement and safety. With real connection, clients are more willing to open up and be transparent.

And what enables that extraordinary rapport? What a coincidence, emotional intelligence. Social awareness and relationship management are expressions of your emotional intelligence that enable extraordinary rapport. So get the sequence of this. First you connect to yourself. That's critical. Then you connect to them - also critical. The combination of those things is irreplaceable, unbeatable.

Your Hand Is On The Switch

Here's a simple way to picture connection. Imagine you and one other person and each of you has a big switch your chest, one of those cartoon switches with a big handle. Now imagine the lines of communication flowing from one switch to another. If both switches are open, there is connection that is free flowing and rapport is established. If either switch is closed, there is no connection. When your switch is closed, as in when you are thinking of the future or caught up in an emotional reaction, you can't connect.

If you're disconnected from yourself, you're disconnected from them. To connect first make sure that *your* switch is open, connect with yourself, set aside your judgments and take an active interest in them. Then they will open *their* switch.

Be Contextual

I'm using the term "be contextual" to mean set the context. Context is the environment within which learning occurs and is experienced. So when you're setting the context, when you are being contextual, you are shaping the learning environment. Let's say that you wanted the context of your classes to be experienced as safe and inviting. Three ways you could set the context would be:

1. Set aside all judgment and be totally accepting of everyone.

2. Demonstrate that all questions are welcome and that there is no such thing as a dumb question.

3. Give people permission to participate in whatever way is comfortable for them.

You set context with your behavior and with the agreements you make that are both specific and implied. Your ability to set the context is enabled by your ability to be present and connected.

When you are present, you are in a way saying, "I am going to focus on you and really pay attention." When you really connect you are in a way saying, "I care, I'm interested and I intend to have a quality relationship with you."

Presence, connection and context are interrelated.

What disables your ability to set context, and to be present and to be connected, is a lack of ability to demonstrate emotional intelligence in your behavior.

So, your goal, if you wish to produce the most positive results with your influence, is to become more masterful with your own emotional intelligence.

Now don't let this intimidate you. I'm not saying you won't be a coach or a trainer until you're a master of emotional intelligence. You don't have to be a master or a guru to be an effective coach or facilitator. But what is required is make a commitment to your own continuous development and to be as present and connected as possible.

Remember, you are the influential difference. How do you want to influence today?

About you, the influential difference - what you need to:

Know

✓ You are the influential difference in learning, change and growth. That is true about the facilitator of any subject, but it is especially true in the development of emotional intelligence.

✓ Your way of being, the nature and quality of your behavior, has the single greatest influence on outcomes in your training and your coaching.

✓ The three ways you must be to most powerfully influence learning outcomes are: be present, be connected, be contextual.

Have

✓ Emotional skills that enable presence and connection, including emotional self-awareness, and emotional self-management are critical to staying present.

Do

✓ Stay present to your own experience while coaching or training.

✓ Be in a relationship of extraordinary rapport with your client to create trust, engagement and safety.

✓ Shape the learning environment and the learning experience by choice, through the manner of your behavior and in the agreements you make, both specific and implied.

Chapter 18: What About Coach Certification

Do I need to be certified to be a coach? That is a frequently asked question and of course the answer is no. You don't need to be certified to coach people or to be a successful coach. And, you may want to be certified for other reasons.

The two most prominent organizations that provide coach accreditation are: *The International Coach Federation (ICF)* and *The International Association for Coaching. (IAC)* Each organization provides coach certification but with very different requirements. As of this writing, the biggest differences in certification criteria between the two are:

1. **An Approved Curriculum:** ICF requires you to graduate a coaching school with an ICF approved curriculum.

2. **Required Hours of Experience:** ICF requires you accumulate a minimum number of hours of coaching experience and hours of being coached by an ICF mentor coach.

3. **Coaching Masteries:** IAC requires only that you demonstrate knowledge and ability in nine coaching competencies (they call them masteries) by passing a written and verbal test. The verbal test requires that you submit two recordings of you coaching an actual client. The recordings are adjudicated. Getting a passing grade on both certifies you as a coach.

There are a number of coaching schools that also offer their own school certification, independent of IAC or ICF credentialing. For example: EQ At Work, the coaching school I founded, provides certification as an emotional intelligence coach, independent of IAC or ICF credentialing, and also prepares candidates for IAC certification.

You will find many choices in coach training. In searching the Internet, I found over 300 coaching schools listed.

People argue for and against coach certification. The arguments *for* coach certification include:

- ✓ Establishing professional credibility
- ✓ Adhering to a standard code of ethics
- ✓ Participating in coach specific training
- ✓ Receiving expert training in coaching specialties like emotional intelligence.

The main argument *against* certification is usually that it is not necessary.

> **I think the main value in the certification process is participating in the required learning and practice activities to achieve coaching mastery. Masterful coaching is more than just a conversation or encouragement.**

The more masterful you are as a coach the more effective you will be and capable of empowering others to extraordinary results.

About Credibility

The ICF website recently cited the results of a survey of their members that shows that 52% of members reported that they had been asked for coaching credentials by clients. I am willing to speculate that result is uniquely influenced by ICF membership.

In more than 15 years of coaching I have never been asked once for credentials, and I have worked with some high profile clients. Your competence, confidence and leadership are what clients want. If they experience that in your presence, you will be very credible and they will want to hire you.

I have observed, in interviewing many coach candidates that many want to be certified in order to "feel" credible. I can't predict what will happen with certification in the future. Perhaps it will be imposed, but I think that would be very difficult because coaching has grown beyond a specialty profession to a business service offered by a wide variety of experts - not just those doing life or business coaching as described by the IAC or ICF.

You make the choice. If you want to complete certification training because you are determined to achieve mastery, fine. If you want to be part of an association of professionals for support, fine. But, be aware if you are choosing to be certified in order to "feel" credible. Build your own credibility with you by being authentic.

About coach certification what you need to:

Know

- ✓ You do not need to be certified to be a coach.

- ✓ Coach certification can offer you advantages, especially in developing necessary skills.

- ✓ The certification requirements of both major certifying organizations do identify essential coaching skills.

Have

- ✓ A clear understanding of what your objectives and needs are in coaching and training, and how certification may serve you.

Do

- ✓ Build your confidence and credibility from within and don't expect certification will do that for you.

- ✓ Examine the coaching competencies required for certification and develop them. You will be a better coach.

- ✓ If you choose a coaching school find one that will best prepare you for the type of coaching you plan to do.

Chapter 19: A Successful EQ Coaching Career?

Can I Earn A Good Living As An EQ Coach?

Well I guess that's the $64,000 question or the $150,000 question. I don't know what your requirements are but you can earn as much as you want and need. It is common for me to be asked, "Can I be successful as an EQ coach?" That depends on your definition of success. Here's mine:

Success in coaching is:

1. Providing extraordinarily effective coaching.

2. Having all the clients you want and need.

3. Becoming more self-realized and fulfilled.

You can have that success if that is your intention.

Providing extraordinarily effective coaching, with emotional intelligence, is the result of your ability to demonstrate essential coach competencies and your ability to facilitate a development process that creates lasting beneficial change of behavior.

Of course you can have all the clients you want and need if you are ready to use best practices and accept that level of success. To run a successful coaching business you will need to learn and do the marketing things that successful coaches do.

But the absolute best way to be successful is to be that which you are teaching. You do not need to be a guru, but if you can, demonstrate being authentic and present, you will attract business like a magnet, while enjoying extraordinary personal satisfaction.

Earnings per hour vary, coach to coach, based on their local market, and their coaching experience and expertise, but mostly on their own internal experience of their value. Hourly rates for an EQ coach range from $75 per hour to $500 an hour. And yes, it is quite possible to reach the level of financial success many regard as the benchmark for truly successful coaches - $150,000 per year. The money you earn is a result of your commitment, and focus.

Have A Focus - Solve Problems

You will be more successful as an emotional intelligence coach if you have a specific coaching focus and if your coaching solves a problem. Yes, you will find some clients who will be attracted to work with you because you are an emotional intelligence coach, but more will come to get their specific needs met. People don't necessarily buy emotional intelligence they buy a solution to a problem, or support to reach a goal. Find your specialty.

For example: I specialized in leadership emotional intelligence and was very successful at attracting business from major organizations throughout the US and Canada.

Which unique application of emotional intelligence would you like to specialize in? It could be: parenting emotional intelligence, high performance teams, entrepreneur emotional intelligence, or something else. Think about how you can leverage your strengths, knowledge and experience in your emotional intelligence coaching or training offerings.

To be successful as an EQ coach you need to:

Know

✓ What success is for you.

Have

✓ A clear focus on whom you are serving, how you best serve them and why.

Be

- ✓ Committed to your own learning.
- ✓ A demonstration of what you are teaching.

Chapter 20: How EQ Improves Coaching And Training Results

How can emotional intelligence improve your coaching and training results?

Are you already a coach, consultant or trainer who has had some success, but you want to take yourself and your clients to the next level? You can improve your coaching and training results doing one, or both, of two things – 1. Develop *your own* EQ to be a more emotionally intelligent coach and/or 2. Be an emotional intelligence coach and develop *your client's* EQ.

What is success in client results?

How would you define success in coaching or training? Some say it is when the client has an "aha moment" and "the light comes on in their eyes." Others say it is when they actually learn something. I say, insight and learning are great but unless they are combined with action nothing happens.

Perhaps you, as I do, recognize that the client's coaching or training has been successful when the client is empowered - when they become more confident, take charge of their life and work, and change for the better.

> **Clients are able to make positive change when they gain deep insight into their behaviors and experience the effect of those behaviors. And, when they become motivated, recognize new options, and take purposeful action.**

How will developing your client's EQ help them achieve success?

Clients are emotional beings. If they understand how emotions are moving them and learn to manage themselves, they suddenly have more options. They are no longer stuck with their habitual reactions but are free to make new choices and take new actions. With emotional information they can address the cause of their behavior and not just the affect.

For example, as discussed in Chapter 3: Core EI Skills, if a client wants to become better at time management she can address the symptoms - being late to meetings, forgetting appointments, or not meeting commitments - with new tools or techniques. She can get a new calendar program or, tie a string around her finger to help her remember.

> **Or, using emotional intelligence, she can address the emotional causes of her time management overwhelm - like not being able to say no and overcommitting when she fears rejection and can't deal with the way she feels.**

When clients have developed the skills of self-awareness and self-management and now command their authentic power, they can use the skills of social awareness and relationship management to positively influence others and get things done. For example, our time management client can gain insight into the emotional needs of her clients and collaborate to create realistic schedules.

With less energy wasted on resisting emotional experience and in avoiding difficult working relationships, your clients will also experience less stress and greater ease.

How will developing your EQ improve the results you get with your coaching and training clients?

The more you develop your emotional intelligence the more effective you will be as a coach and trainer!

How you are being while you are doing coaching and training makes the greatest difference in your effectiveness and your client results, as I described in Chapter 17: The Influential Difference. With greater command of emotional skills you will be more present, connected and able to set context to shape a more powerful and effective learning experience. In fact, your emotional intelligence will improve your coaching and training in dozens of ways. A good example is what I call "the coachable moment."

The Coachable Moment

In coaching there are times when the client reveals him or herself unconsciously in something they say or something they don't say. It is typically a moment of dissonance. In response to a question they might say, "No that doesn't bother me at all." But your emotional, visceral experience is quite different and the subtext of their speech seems to be, "That really affects me but I'm not gonna show it." That is a coachable moment. There is something potentially important behind that dissonance that if explored could yield important insight. And if it is not explored it will continue to dominate the space, but in the background. And that can prevent the rest of the coaching session from being effective.

To be an extraordinarily effective coach you must be able to recognize and act on these opportunities as they arise. Simple you say? But, you might be amazed at how often I have observed in my mentor coaching that the coachable moment is passed up - by new and experienced coaches alike. How does that happen?

What Happens?

Coachable moments are passed up when the coach is more concerned with surviving the moment than coaching.

The coach may be anxious about being able to serve the client and look good doing it. They are trying hard to think of the next thing to say or do that will add value.

Coachable moments are passed up when a coach is afraid to ask a question, or challenge the client - thinking either "I should know what that means" or "I don't want to risk offending."

Sometimes coaches avoid engaging in those moment because they unconsciously sense the importance of what has been said or left unsaid, but are afraid they can't handle it.

Emotional Blind Spots

In preparation for some of my mentor coaching I listen to actual coaching sessions, recorded with the client's permission. In the mentor coaching session I ask the coach, "did you notice when *that thing* happened?" (When the client said or did that) "Well yes," they often say, "I did think that was a little odd but I didn't know what to say or do and I felt uncomfortable about going there, so we went on." When I explore further with the coach, "uncomfortable" usually means: "it brought up emotions *in me* that I didn't want to deal with" or "when the client did that, I did not want to deal with *their* emotions."

Sometimes when I ask about what I observed was a coachable moment, the coach will say, "Gosh no. That just went right by me." Later when they go back and listen to the recording again and notice how obvious the dissonance in the situation was, they are surprised.

Why didn't the coach notice? For the same reasons - they were not able to tolerate the emotional experience and went temporarily unconscious.

Trust me on this one. I observe this all the time in mentor coaching. OK so maybe it doesn't happen to you much. Or maybe it does. This is not an indictment but an invitation. Give yourself permission to consider there are missed opportunities and commit yourself to finding some. I guarantee you will. Then, if you are motivated, what do you do?

Develop Your Emotional Skills

There are several EQ skills that enable you to be most effective in this example situation:

✓ The ability to recognize one's own emotional state and the effect it is having on one's thoughts and choices.

✓ The ability to sustain an experience of one's own emotions, without avoidance yet without being compelled to react.

✓ The ability to recognize the emotions of others and gain deep insight and understanding.

✓ The ability to "be with" the emotions of another without avoidance yet without being compelled to react.

When you as a coach are able to demonstrate these skills to a higher level, you will be able to be present to the coachable moment and will be better able to support the client to greater self-insight and more purposeful choices.

Don't Underestimate The Challenge

"Of course," you say. "I know that." Thanks for reminding me Joseph. I'll be on the lookout for those situations."

Take heed. We are expert at avoiding our feelings. We are so practiced at it that it takes very powerful concentration to get past our own blind spots and internal resistance.

If you are serious about gaining mastery you will need to adopt a very specific practice for improvement.

There's no doubt that developing greater emotional intelligence will improve results for both the client and the coach. If you have a passion for the subject and want to help others develop their EQ, you may want to become certified as an EQ coach.

And, if you are a coach or trainer and you don't plan on coaching others in the development of their emotional intelligence, you, as others have, will certainly discover that EQ Coach certification training not only improves your client's results but sets you free to be happier and more fulfilled.

Regarding how emotional intelligence improves client results, what you need to:

Know

- ✓ Clients are able to make positive change when they gain deep insight into their behaviors and experience the effect of those behaviors. And, when they become motivated, recognize new options, and take purposeful action.

- ✓ Clients are emotional beings. If they understand how emotions are moving them and learn to manage themselves, they suddenly have more options.

- ✓ The more you develop your emotional intelligence the more effective you will be as a coach and trainer!

Have

- ✓ Realistic expectations on the need for your development. We are all expert at avoiding our feelings. We are so practiced at it that it takes very powerful concentration to get past our own blind spots and internal resistance.

- ✓ Specific practices for improvement.

Do

- ✓ Define success for yourself and for your coaching or training clients.

- ✓ Make your coaching more effective and your life easier and more fulfilling by developing your EQ.

Chapter 21: What Is The Best Development Approach For You?

Whether you are an HR professional, internal coach, consultant or trainer, hopefully you have found, in this book, some valuable things to consider in preparing yourself to develop emotional intelligence in individuals and groups. Only you can decide which personal and professional and organizational EQ development path is right for you. A good place to start is by considering your goals for yourself and your clients.

What do you want for your clients?

In one of my coaching classes I asked the students, "What is your goal for your clients? What do you want them to get as a result of your coaching?" Some of the answers were: "I want them to have some Aha! Moments," and, "I want them to think differently about their life and work," and, "I want to inspire them and have them see new possibilities."

"Those are great answers," I told them, "and I'd like those things too, but they are not my real goal for coaching."

My real goal for coaching is to empower my clients to be as effective, successful and happy, as they would like, by adopting new habits of behavior that create new positive results.

What do you want for your employees or your internal or external clients? Do you want them to think differently about emotional intelligence or do you want them to behave differently?

If lasting beneficial change of behavior is what you are after, your development approach will be different than one you would take to just have your people be inspired and think differently about emotional intelligence.

What are your goals for yourself?

Whether you are an experienced coach or just setting out to be a coach, emotional intelligence offers some wonderful opportunity - if it is right for you. Consider what attracts you to coaching emotional intelligence. Do you feel a special connection to the subject? Perhaps you have had some success making your own life changes by working with your emotions. Maybe you have done some emotional work with others as a counselor and want to make it your specialty but prefer to do it in a coaching relationship. Ask yourself:

- How will coaching emotional intelligence fulfill my purpose?

- What is my commitment to my own continuing development? For example: Is personal growth a part of your lifestyle or would you like it to be? Is it your intention to become more self-realized and fulfilled? do you have the desire and the discipline to develop new skills? If the answers to these questions are yes, EQ is a wonderful vehicle for you.

- Do I want to be an emotional intelligence coach, do I simply want to be more emotionally intelligent, or both?

What are your development goals for your organization?

Whether you are a coach, consultant, internal trainer or HR specialist, ask yourself:

- What are the organization's goals?

- Do we want to transform the culture to be an emotionally intelligent workplace? Or do we just want to promote some new skills?

- What level of development do I want to provide? What's my ultimate objective, introduction or change? Which is more important to me training or entertaining? Which do I most want to provide, information or transformation?

For your purpose, you may be satisfied with a very basic approach – you may only want to introduce the concepts of emotional intelligence in your organization, build a little awareness and let people take it further on their own. You will probably find that a lighter training approach, the use of video, and perhaps a short workshop is sufficient to your purpose. You can certainly use some of the ideas in this book and there are many other resources to support your effort.

Perhaps you are really committed to being a change agent. If that is true, you will find emotional intelligence a great tool to empower people to be their most powerful and creative self and you will want a more in-depth approach to developing yourself and your clients that includes training, coaching and support over time.

> **For example, I believe that the measure of success in any development program is lasting beneficial change of behavior. To that end I have always approached learning as a process and not just an event, and my development programs have always included a blend of training, coaching and self-practice over time. Is that an approach you would like for you and your clients?**

We all have a unique and wonderful opportunity to make a difference, in our organizations and in our world, and in doing so experience extraordinary fulfillment. It is fulfilling, for example, to teach someone how to use their emotions effectively instead of being compelled by their emotions. It is hugely satisfying to empower people to break limiting habits and enjoy better and more productive workplace relationships. And I have found it extraordinarily satisfying to help people use EQ to become more self-realized.

> **When learning EQ, years ago, it became clear to me that emotional skill was valuable but not the real prize. I recognized that the process of increasing one's emotional skill creates an opportunity to claim the greatest benefit of developing emotional intelligence - the ability to access and express one's most authentically powerful, creative and happy self - as a leader, an individual and a human being.**

What do you imagine our world would be like if more people had more highly developed emotional intelligence? I see emotional intelligence development as a means of transforming global consciousness resulting in a peaceful and sustainable existence for all. And I believe that you, as an emotional intelligence coach and trainer, are a potent force for that transformation.

Whatever your path, it has been my pleasure to support you, provoke your thinking and to share some information and experience to help you prepare for your next step. Please help yourself to the additional resources found in the appendix of this book.

To your health, and an emotionally intelligent and happy life!

Joseph Liberti

Appendix: Assessments and Resources

Core Emotional Skills Assessment

This simple questionnaire lists ten core emotional skills. It is not scientifically validated and is not intended to be an absolute measure of your emotional intelligence, but is useful in recognizing your present level of competence and setting goals for your development. Be as objective and realistic as you can be. Print your results and save them. Later you can complete a second questionnaire (or several) and evaluate your progress.

To complete the EQ At Work Core Emotional Skills Questionnaire go to:

http://www.eqatwork.com/emotional-skills-assessment

To download the guide to using the assessment and tips for improvement go to:

http://www.eqatwork.com/coach/josephliberti/cee-1-book-downloads

This will help you understand your scoring and give you tips to improve your skill.

Your special password for both is 123eqatwork4me

Readiness Checklist

How ready are you to launch your emotional intelligence development initiative or coaching career? What do you need to do next?

To support you I have created a checklist: The 30 most important things you need to know, have or do to be successful in coaching and training emotional intelligence. The 30 items will help you evaluate your readiness and your progress.

Use the checklist to:

- Assess your readiness to coach emotional intelligence.

- Evaluate your preparation for launching a program.

- Gain clarity on your intended development outcomes

- Prepare for your own success and the success of your clients.

To download The 30 Most Important Things Checklist go to:

http://www.eqatwork.com/coach/josephliberti/cee-1-book-downloads

EQ At Work Coach Certification News

Subscribe and get news and schedules of the EQ At Work Certification programs, and tips on coaching and presentation at

http://www.eqatwork.com

EQ At Work Coach Certification Program

To learn more about training the EQ At Work EQ Coach and Trainer Certification Program visit: http://www.eqatwork.com/coach-certification